"ALL-AMERICAN GIRL"

"ALL-AMER

ICAN GIRL"

The Art of
Coles Phillips

by Michael Schau

WATSON-GUPTILL PUBLICATIONS/NEW YORK

Copyright © 1975 by Watson-Guptill Publications
First published 1975 in New York by Watson-Guptill Publications,
a division of Billboard Publications, Inc.,
One Astor Plaza, New York, N.Y. 10036

Manufactured in U.S.A.

Library of Congress Cataloging in Publication Data
Schau, Michael, 1945–
    All-American girl.
    Includes index.
    1.   Phillips, Coles, 1880–1927.   I.   Phillips,
Coles, 1880–1927.   II.   Title.
NC139.P43S32   741.9'73   75-12697
ISBN 0–8230–0173–3

First Printing, 1975

Edited by Susan Davis
Designed by James Craig and Bob Fillie
Set in 14 point Goudy by Gerard Associates/Graphics Art, Inc.
Printed by Parish Press, Inc., New York
Bound by A. Horowitz and Son, Inc., New York

Again, for Carole

Acknowledgments

It has taken Americans several decades to rediscover our heritage of great illustration. Over those years pictures have disappeared or fallen into disrepair, and information on the artists has been lost. Only through the efforts of many people has this retrospective look at the work of Coles Phillips and a brief biography been made possible.

Among those who so generously shared their pictures, information, and memories are Jane and Stephen Klain, Walter Kelly, Ugo Mochi, Mrs. William Bruce, Hanson W. Baldwin, Greg Smith, Vincent Petragnani, Stanley S. Newcomb, Dr. Myles Gombert, Professor William Jefferies of the U.S. Naval Academy, June Schetterer at the New Rochelle *Standard-Star*, Thomas B. Greenslade of Kenyon College, The New York Public Library, the New Rochelle Public Library, the Springfield (Ohio) Public Library, and especially Joseph and Nancy Suess.

Special thanks is due Mrs. Helen Eddy of Saybrook, Connecticut, who is Coles Phillips' sister.

Grateful acknowledgment is expressed to several companies for which Phillips did advertising work: Oneida Ltd. Silversmiths, Norwich Pharmacal Company, Jantzen, Inc., Clark Equipment Company, *Good Housekeeping* magazine, and Pratt & Lambert, Inc.

All material from the old *Life* magazine was made available through the courtesy of Mr. Henry T. Rockwell.

Watson-Guptill Publications has done much to fill a void in America's cultural history with its books on American illustration. Donald Holden, Editorial Director, had the imagination to see promise in a book on Coles Phillips, and Assistant Editorial Director Diane Hines made many useful suggestions while getting the project underway. Editor Susan Davis's contributions have been invaluable in matters of both pictures and text.

The pictures by Phillips are the very heart of this book. American illustration in the early part of this century was ephemeral; many of the printed decorations by Phillips, as well as his original works, have been lost. This book has been dedicated to photographer Carole Schau, who is not incidentally my wife, for her contribution in presenting Phillips' work. Not only did she do 90 percent of the black and white photography, but she spent scores of hours restoring the works, covering the scars of old age to make the pictures—all of them 50 to 70 years old—appear as Phillips painted them. It is through her talent and energy that this book is made possible.

Contents

Color Plates

Introduction

Coles Phillips, 1911.

DURING the Golden Age of Illustration, the name and art of Coles Phillips ranked alongside the great illustrative artists of the day. The "Phillips Girl" became as popular with the American public as those images created by Charles Dana Gibson and Harrison Fisher, his pictures as instantly recognizable as those of his best fellow artists — Maxfield Parrish, Howard Chandler Christy, James Montgomery Flagg, J.C. Leyendecker, and Norman Rockwell.

Coles Phillips' position in the forefront of American illustration is a fact, but his art cannot be discussed in the same context as that of his contemporaries. Like many illustrators who glorified a particular aspect of American life — rural innocence, urban sophistication, the Gay Nineties — Phillips painted the ideal image of American womanhood. But he was far more interested in graphic design than subject matter. Phillips painted dream girls, fantasy women, an already-universal subject, but through imaginative design—the very heart of any Phillips picture—he created his own special view of American women as well.

Phillips was also unique in that he started an art career later in life than his famous contemporaries and made an extraordinary success without the benefit of formal art study. He regretted his lack of training, but it is surely that untutored, natural instinct for picture design that made him popular and his pictures accepted internationally. The public whole-heartedly appreciated Coles Phillips' art.

Clarence Coles Phillips was born in Springfield, Ohio, the son of Jason and Anna Size Phillips, in October 1880. (The exact date is unknown since no records were kept before 1890; children were born at home and there are no records of christenings.) Both parents were of prominent and prosperous Springfield familes, and Jason managed the family clothing business. The Phillipses lived at 107 North Limestone Street when Clarence was born, the third of four children. His brother Frank and sister Ann were 12 and 10 years older, respectively, and his sister Helen was born in 1884. The family moved to Washington, D.C., briefly during 1885, but within months returned to Springfield and settled at 580 East High Street, where the Phillipses remained as long as the family lived in one household.

Coles disliked his given name and never used it, preferring to be called Cy by his family and close friends. He was a handsome child, shorter than average, popular, and spoiled by a doting mother. He sang with the High Street Methodist Church Choir, kept pet pigeons, and worked at the neighborhood grocery after school. In every respect he had a normal, healthy boyhood.

As is the case with most artists, young Cy showed a precocious talent for drawing. Family and neighbors recall he drew constantly and entertained friends with caricatures and quick sketches of animals. The boy's talent for drawing seems to have gone unnoticed by his family except for an uncle, Jerome Uhl, a German immigrant and painter who married Jason Phillips' sister Mattie. Uhl became one of Ohio's foremost portrait artists, with pictures of local politicians his speciality. During a family reunion in 1892, Uhl saw some of the sketches done by his nephew and encouraged his parents to develop the talent.

EVIDENTLY the Phillipses ignored the advice because Cy's early training amounted to what little guidance he received at public school. His parents were conservative and, no doubt, found art a distasteful occupation for their son. They had guided their eldest, Frank, into law and later Ann would go to Vassar. When Helen, Cy's younger sister, studied singing and became good enough to work for a career on the concert stage, it was Mrs. Phillips who found a way to put an end to those ambitions.

Had Cy wanted passionately to study art, he probably could have persuaded his mother to allow it. Even as a youngster he was able to manipulate his mother and his friends to give him his way. He had a winning personality, reinforced by an intense stare, which he found adequate compensation for his lack of height. A neighbor of the Phillips family remembers Coles as "extremely handsome, one of the handsomest men in Springfield. Very blonde with sharp blue eyes. He had a long thin face and all of the women were crazy about him. I would even say quite a few girls were in love with him."

If the boy thought of a future career at all, it may have been in music. His tenor voice enjoyed an outstanding reputation in Springfield. A musical group for which he was lead singer entertained at the many functions befitting the son of a local businessman. And he was often cast as the star of musicales.

Still Coles never abandoned his interest in drawing. Beginning in 1897 when he was at Springfield High School, he did some illustration work for *The American,* a weekly magazine published in Springfield. If he considered an art career, it was natural that he would turn to graphic arts. The western Ohio town had no art museum, so Coles had little exposure there to painting and sculpture. But book and magazine illustrations were everywhere, and it was natural that they would attract his attention. Work of the best illustrators of the day was available for the boy's admiration and emulation.

ON GRADUATION from high school, Coles thought about entering art school in New York City, but his father wanted him to go to college and study business. Mr. Phillips probably hoped that his energetic son could help build up the clothing store, which was not doing well. In what must have been the result of a stalemate between father and son, as well as the need to earn tuition, Coles went to work in 1900 for the American Radiator Company in Springfield. The family friend Stanley DeLong took the boy under his wing and gave him a job as a clerk. But Phillips was obviously ill-suited for clerical work:

"Clarence had an attractive personality," DeLong said later of his employee, "but he wasn't fitted for business. I had one of those high desks at which one sat on a stool, and Clarence had a low, flat-topped desk right behind me. He was always behind in his work. I don't think he ever really did catch up with it. When I would turn around and look down at his desk, there he would be drawing while his work waited. I told him he would never make good in the kind of work he was doing. He admitted it and said the only kind of work he cared about was drawing."

Clerking at American must have convinced Coles that college was preferable; he enrolled in 1901 at Kenyon College in Gambier, Ohio. He was a competent student, carrying a "B" average his first year, and his outgoing style made him as popular in college as he had been in his hometown. He joined Alpha Delta Phi fraternity (his fraternity brothers quickly nicknamed him "Psi") and made friends there who would last a lifetime. Even when he became a celebrated artist in New York, he continued to participate in Alpha Delta Phi functions.

Most important, Kenyon gave Coles an excellent audience for his drawing talent. Editors of the school newspaper and the yearbook, *The Reveille*, used his illustrations (page 49) during the three years he was at Kenyon. Boredom with working his way through college and the success of his drawings made him even more determined to pursue a career in art, so he decided after his Junior year to leave Kenyon and Ohio, and go to New York to study art.

Kenyon College gave Phillips the opportunity to do illustrations for the yearbook *The Reveille*. In 1908, four years after he left Kenyon, Coles designed the cover for *Songs of Kenyon*, a collection of school songs. Photo Thomas Greenslade.

COLES PHILLIPS arrived in New York City in the summer of 1904 and settled in a rooming house on 34th Street. He shared lodgings for a time with an old friend from Springfield, Wilbur Cummings, a clerk in a Wall Street law office. Bringing with him a letter of recommendation from his former boss, Mr. DeLong, at American Radiator, he took a job with American's New York office to support himself. For some reason plans to enter the Art Students League never materialized. Maybe he wasn't able to afford the tuition, or perhaps he applied and was not accepted.

Coles made more of a success his second time at American, and he rose quickly from clerk to salesman. But selling heating equipment still had little allure for the young man, and his favorite office pastime was, as always, drawing. He could succeed at anything that he felt was worthy of his energy, but evidently banal office work wasn't among these.

His career with the company came to an abrupt end within months. Once again his art was the cause. He and a co-worker were in the men's lavatory, complaining about the company president. Coles took an envelope from his pocket and began to sketch a rather rude caricature of the executive. Unfortunately when they emerged from the men's room and the friend showed the picture to co-workers, the president was standing nearby. He demanded to see the picture, and the young men were dismissed on the spot.

That evening Coles' friend had dinner with John Ames Mitchell, editor of the humor magazine *Life*. He told the story of how he had been fired that day and showed the caricature to Mitchell. The editor thought the picture clever and told the man to send Phillips around to his office with some of his drawings. He might find a place for them in the pages of *Life*.

Such coincidences are the stuff of artists' fantasies. But that it should actually happen to Coles so soon after his arrival in New York is astonishing. Even more astonishing is that the budding artist did not take advantage of Mitchell's invitation. He acted as though he had supreme self-confidence, but in reality working for the top humor magazine of the day must have seemed outside the realm of possibility.

It is likely that this lack of confidence in his artistic abilities — a feeling that would haunt him throughout his life — pushed Coles to seek training. He enrolled in a night class at the Chase School of Art, which appears to be the school run by the portraitist William Merritt Chase (not to be confused with the school opened later by the other portraitist Joseph Cummings Chase). He took extra classes in watercolor at the Free School on 44th Street.

During the day Phillips went to work for a studio that turned out pictures for menswear catalogs. An assembly-line operation employing men who could do only hack work, it was certainly no place to develop as an artist. Illustrators, each specializing in one portion of the figure, sat at one long table. One would paint the suit and turn over the picture to another who did the head, another shoes, and so on. Coles tolerated this position for two months and left the "fashion factory" to seek a job with an advertising agency. He also chose not to reenroll for classes at Chase and the Free School. The three months' training there would be the sum of his formal art studies.

PURE BRAVADO secured Phillips his next position. He brought a portfolio of his drawings and watercolors to the offices of a large advertising agency. "My name is Coles Phillips and I am going to work for you," he announced. In later years he enjoyed telling of this brash introduction. The sketches proffered were crudely done, but the manager saw in them the same vitality and assurance that the artist exuded. Coles Phillips was obviously an appealing man with a forceful personality. He was hired.

The company was far from the sophisticated sales organization an ad agency is today. The firm served more as an artists' clearing house for companies wishing to buy promotional pictures. Coles' confidence in selling his own work there proved an asset, and he was quickly promoted from staff artist to artist-client liaison. He had little time to create pictures of his own, but Coles learned firsthand the workings of the agency, and he soon realized that he could operate a similar office of his own. Within a year he had saved enough money to do just that.

The C.C. Phillips & Company Agency opened in 1906 in small, bare offices at 27 East 22nd Street. The young entrepreneur asked two staff artists with whom he worked to join him in the venture. The company was moderately successful, mainly because of Phillips' back-breaking work. His responsibility and schedule were exhausting. Phillips would call on clients at their offices, make sketches and some completed pictures for campaigns, oversee his assistants' work, and manage the office. During the period he seldom returned to his 34th Street rooms with less than a 16-hour day behind him.

However, the modest success of the agency did not please Coles. He had hoped to make a career as an artist, and once again, he found that his attempt to combine art and business forced his painting to suffer. He was determined to be a painter, even if the new agency must be abandoned.

Since that seemed his only choice, he found jobs at other companies for his two cohorts and searched for a studio for himself. Closing the C.C. Phillips Agency in early 1907 left Coles money enough to pay expenses and live for one month. He would have to make good as an artist in thirty days.

In February he saw a newspaper ad for an artist's studio at 13 West 29th Street. He must have been a forceful salesman or the landlord was naive about young artists, for he let the studio to Phillips on the promise that the rent would be paid at the end of the month. Phillips said that he had orders for pictures, but was unable to pay until they were completed. Armed with the hopes of making his tale a reality, and with an easel willed to him by his late uncle, Jerome Uhl, he went to work.

The situation was far from hopeless since Phillips had a plan of attack. He had given considerable thought to John Ames Mitchell's invitation to submit work to *Life* magazine. In the intervening two years, Coles studied the magazine's drawings and covers, and he decided his own work could fit into that format.

WITH THE SELF-IMPOSED deadline prodding him, Coles spent long days in the small studio sketching, experimenting with endless ideas for cartoons. Still, nothing seemed fine enough for America's foremost humor magazine. One evening after another unsuccessful day, Coles went to the German Village, a neighborhood tavern. There he saw two women sitting at a table in the ladies' section — a pretty young woman sharing a bottle of wine with a very old woman. Suddenly the younger woman raised her glass and proposed a toast to her companion. The scene delighted Coles and he grabbed his sketch pad. He even persuaded the older woman to pose for more complete sketches.

Phillips worked to develop the picture, drawing and redrawing it in the few days he had left. This subject would be right for *Life*, he was sure. With the thirty days of his allotted time almost at an end, he completed the cartoon. But he had trouble thinking of a caption for it and asked friends for advice. Even his landlord, who had a proprietary interest in the finished product, could not think of a clever title. Finally, Coles decided on a quote from the "The Rubaiyat of Omar Khayyam" — "The Cup That Clears Today of Past Regrets and Future Fears."

With the single picture tucked under his arm, Phillips walked to the Life Building, a few blocks away at 17 West 31st Street. He asked to see John

Ames Mitchell. A young assistant informed the artist that the editor, who personally selected all art for *Life*, saw pictures on Wednesdays only. Moved by dwindling resources and visions of his angry landlord, Phillips was persistent. The bored young assistant was equally adamant.

Gerald Krone, one of *Life*'s business managers, who was passing through the office on his way to talk with Mitchell, saw the cartoon and suggested that the chief would probably like to see the picture. Krone himself took the drawing into his meeting with Mitchell. Within minutes word was sent out: "Mr. Mitchell will see Mr. Phillips." If Coles Phillips had ever sold an idea to anyone, he had better do it now!

"I don't remember seeing your work before. Is this a flash in the pan or can you do more work as good?" Mitchell asked.

Coles assured the editor of his ability and left the office with a check for $150 for his first picture and a request for more. C. Coles Phillips was now a magazine illustrator.

Coles Phillips' first drawing for *Life* magazine, April 11, 1907. Photo Carole Schau.

WITH THAT TRANSACTION Coles began an association with *Life* that would last the twenty years of his career, and in John Mitchell he found a loyal friend. Mitchell founded *Life* in 1883, and it was his genius as an editor that made it the top humor magazine in America for three decades. Mitchell began as an artist, having studied painting and architecture in Paris for seven years. He illustrated books of verse, wrote short stories, and was a prolific novelist (*The Silent War, Amos Judd, The Pines of Lory,* among others). With a solid background in art and writing, he launched *Life* and cultivated its excellence until his death in 1918.

A short, rotund gentleman with thick spectacles and a Vandyke beard, Mitchell was especially cordial and encouraging to his artists. More than once he created a "star" illustrator because he could see in a roughly drawn picture the promise of finer work. In 1885 he discovered and developed Charles Dana Gibson, when Gibson thought a career in art was hopeless. Gibson would become *Life*'s most popular artist and later its editor.

In 1907 when Phillips began working for *Life*, Mitchell was anxious to find outstanding "girl artists." Two years before, Gibson, whose name since the 1890s was synonymous with *Life*, left America and his "Gibson Girl" to study in Paris as a serious painter. Although a backlog of "Gibson Girl" drawings kept that image before the public, Mitchell was anxious to replace Gibson by developing other artists who would paint young American womanhood.

The Panic of 1907 played havoc with Gibson's finances, and he was forced to return from Europe and to illustration. Mitchell was delighted to welcome the "Gibson Girl" back to *Life*, but he still wanted more pictures of women from his other artists.

The first cartoon by Coles Phillips appeared in the April 11, 1907, issue. That particular number included an editorial by Mitchell on Theodore Roosevelt's presidential candidacy the following year; a letter from actress Minnie Madden Fiske concerning proper treatment of cattle; a review of a new melodrama, "The Ambitious Mrs. Alcott"; and a review of Carl Snyder's book *The World Machine.* There were cartoons poking fun at ballooning, which had become the national craze, and, of course, drawings of lovely young women.

During the winter of 1907–1908, many drawings by the new artist Coles Phillips appeared in *Life*, particularly in the magazine's most prestigious position, the center double-page spread. On February 20, 1908, Phillips' first cover was run. After that introduction to the public, there was a

"Phillips Girl" on *Life*'s cover as often as once each month.

It was fortunate that Phillips was finding success as an artist, for his family in Springfield was having financial difficulties. Mrs. Phillips had inherited large real estate holdings from her mother (the Springfield City Hall is on land once owned by her family), but she lost most of her fortune in the 1890s in land speculation in Kansas. Now, in the faltering economy of 1907, the family business was in serious trouble.

Coles asked his parents and sister Helen to move to New York, with a promise to set them up in an apartment. He also offered to pay for Helen's voice lessons. The three came East, and Coles took an apartment for them in New Rochelle. The town just north of New York City was famous as a community where illustrators and artists lived and worked, and Coles thought it would be more to their liking than Manhattan. He kept his studio on 29th Street, but moved to larger quarters next door at 15 West, and commuted often to New Rochelle. Jason Phillips died in 1908, soon after the move, and Coles' mother remained to keep house for her son.

I N THE SPRING of 1908, Mitchell decided that *Life* would join the growing number of periodicals going to four-color covers. But rather than have his artists produce in color the type of picture they had been doing, he asked his major cover artists — which now included Phillips — to design new types of covers. As an artist and editor Mitchell knew that nothing new in magazine illustration was possible. It had all been done before in one form or another. Still, he was hoping for designs that would be distinctive and decidedly new to *Life*.

Phillips had been working with a particular technique during his advertising agency days that he thought might be adapted to *Life* covers. It was a design in which the main portion of a figure — generally the clothing — blended into the background of the picture. The figure was defined by highlights on hands, face, and legs. The idea came to Coles one evening at a friend's room as he watched the man, dressed in black and playing the violin in dim light. He was suggested only by highlights on his face, shirt front, hands, and violin.

Phillips went to work to apply the technique for a *Life* color cover. Using his sister Helen as a model, he drew a woman feeding chickens. She was in a white polka-dotted dress, and her figure was suggested only by head, arms, and legs. The sketch for this "fade-away" design (as it was popularly called) was submitted to Mitchell, who was excited by it. Mitchell asked Coles

Coles' sister Helen posed for "Corn Exchange," the first fade-away design for *Life* in 1908. This initial fade-away established the technique that became the artist's trademark. Photo Carole Schau.

to complete that watercolor and to submit more "fade-away girls." The first cover with that technique appeared on the May 28, 1908, issue; the initial sketch of the woman feeding chickens ran on a subsequent one. The public grabbed up magazines on which the fade-away was used.

Phillips' first work was accepted by *Life* because he imitated the style and content of Gibson's drawings. Phillips brought a pleasant freshness to several themes that had been Gibson favorites: pretty ladies who used their beauty to hold sway over young men, the foolishness of an old man loving a young woman, the greater foolishness of a young woman loving an old man for his money. But the creation of the fade-away gave Phillips his own technique and the confidence to be first-rate Phillips rather than second-rate Gibson.

If Coles started his career in art later in life than most of his contemporaries, he made up for it by surpassing the success of many of them almost instantaneously. Within one year Phillips' *Life* covers were second in popularity and frequency of appearance only to those of James Montgomery Flagg. By mid-1909 it was not unusual to see several Coles Phillips covers in weekly succession, with drawings inside the same issues. At the end of 1908, just eighteen months after his first drawing appeared, *Life* was issuing reproductions of his covers for sale and as gifts to new subscribers. A 1909 Coles Phillips calendar featuring six of the year's most popular "fade-away girls" was issued. A Phillips calendar would be published each year thereafter for more than a decade. Since *Life* was also known internationally, Coles' cover designs were recognized in England, where sets of Phillips postcards published in London sold widely.

I N 1911 AND 1912, collections of "Phillips Girls" appeared in hardcover books; only the best illustrators of day were worthy of such publications. In 1911 The Century Company published *A Gallery of Girls by Coles Phillips* — forty pictures that had appeared mainly in *Life* and *Good Housekeeping*. The following year Bobbs-Merrill came out with *A Young Man's Fancy*, another collection of Phillips women.

Coles' success is extraordinary when you consider the proliferation of "girl illustrators" at the time. The "Phillips Girl" was in keen competition with pictures of young beauties by Harrison Fisher, Henry Hutt, McClelland Barclay, John LaGatta, Flagg, Gibson, and scores of others. Within a year after the "fade-away girl" appeared, imitators were everywhere. Magazine editors for such periodicals as *Harper's* and *Leslie's Weekly* were asking artists for pictures using the technique, hoping to boost sales the way a Phillips cover could for *Life*. Valentine Sundberg tried his hand at a series of fade-away pictures for *Leslie's*, but they were flat and uninteresting and were soon discontinued. In later years J.C. Leyendecker, one of Phillips' closest friends, made powerful use of black fade-away in cigarette and Arrow Collar advertisements.

The "Phillips Girl" was the logical successor to the "Gibson Girl." Both fade-away and full-figured Phillips women were in the same tradition of idealized women as Gibson's. But Gibson's drawings of svelte, elegant, dignified beauties were born in 1890s' America and firmly rooted in that era. Gibson had painted an age and the passing of that age dated his drawings. He would later attempt to modernize his women, even draw flat-chested, slouching flappers, but his enthusiasm for them was as mild as their impact on the public.

Gibson's pen and inks were masterpieces of black and white, but the "Phillips Girl" had color, both in design and in character. Phillips fleshed out Gibson's young women, made them less elegant, but more saucy, and definitely, if not brazenly, sexy. Gibson painted a young woman's limbs; Phillips painted her legs.

The "Phillips Girl," according to one writer in the introduction to Phillips' *A Young Man's Fancy*, had a unique appeal: "In the drawing room or in the kitchen, breaking hearts or baking pies, or sturdily joying in the mighty stillness of the great outdoors, always alluring, always at home, a real woman from the tip of her dainty boot to the soft glory of her hair, she stands out from her flat background and answers completely to a young man's fancy at its highest and best."

While the description is sappy by any standards, Phillips was truly a romantic artist in a romantic time. And these early pictures show women within the traditionally romantic role — and within editor Mitchell's image of women that he wanted to adorn his magazine. In the pages of *Life*, politics was feared to coarsen women; athletics were agreeable so long as women could be graceful while participating in them. Casual dress was acceptable if gentility and dignity were maintained. Women were idealized by Mitchell and his artists, as well as by most of the "girl illustrators" of the time. Still, many young women of the day tried to live up to the standards painted — impossible as that might be.

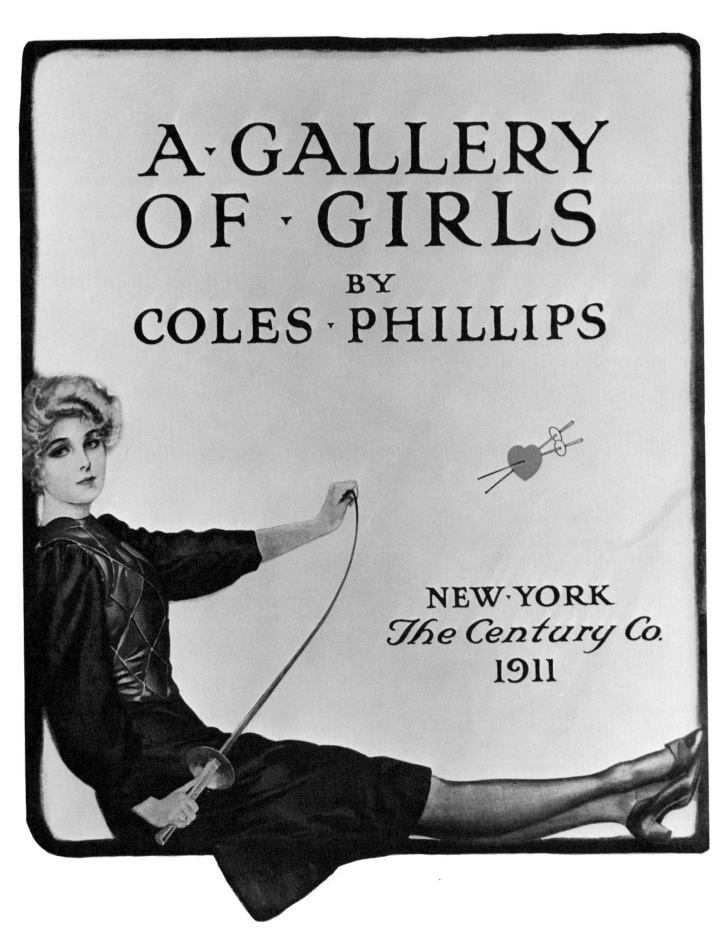

The title page for *A Gallery of Girls by Coles Phillips,* the first published collection of the artist's pictures. Photo Carole Schau.

Coles painted this watercolor portrait of Teresa Hyde in 1909. Photo Carole Schau.

OLES' MOST FREQUENT MODEL during these first successful years was a young nurse, Teresa Hyde, whom he met in December 1907 in front of New York Presbyterian Hospital where she was working. He approached Miss Hyde as he had many other potential models he spotted on the street, at a party, or in a shop: "Hello. I am Coles Phillips, and I would like you to model for a picture." Canadian-born Teresa Hyde was a short, dark, stunningly beautiful woman, and in no time Coles was in love with her. Within months after their meeting, they were engaged, and Teresa was on the cover of *Life*. The March 12, 1908, cover (page 121) is her portrait.

Tess, as her family called her, was only 18 when she met Coles, and already she was a strong-willed young woman. She combined the beauty of a "Phillips Girl" with an independence that he did not often paint into his romanticized figures. Coles had known many women since his arrival in New York, but it was Tess he wanted to marry. Theirs was a long courtship since Phillips needed to wait until he had money enough to support his mother and sister as well as take care of a family of his own. His success at *Life* was financially rewarding, but not what was needed to support two households.

Meanwhile Coles and Tess had a passionate but stormy engagement, interrupted by many arguments. The engagement was broken time and again, but always patched up by one of Coles' friends or his sister Helen. Still, he had no doubt that, despite differences, this was the woman for him. "I would rather have Tess throw plates at me than sit at a meal in harmony with any other woman," he would say. And his feelings proved true, because once they were married, they enjoyed an unusually close relationship.

Phillips began to seek commissions in addition to his work for *Life* in order to save enough to marry. He illustrated books; his first was *Michael Thwaite's Wife* by Miriam Michelson, published by Doubleday in 1909 (page 55). Phillips' women were perfectly suited to illustrate the popular romantic novels of the day. The final paragraph of the Michelson novel is itself the best description of the adult fairy tales that Coles decorated:

"He laughed and the world grew light and livable to her at that low laugh of content. 'We've struck a bargain, Joy,' he said softly. 'I needn't name it, but it's there.' His arm closed about her and he drew her to him. 'Thank God for blindness, my wife! It has given you back to me.'"

Also in 1909 he illustrated *Cords of Vanity* by James Branch Cabell (page

56), whose numerous books were usually illustrated by Howard Pyle. In 1910 Phillips did the illustrations for E. F. Benson's *The Fascinating Mrs. Halton*, published by Grosset & Dunlap (page 55).

Finally, in the early part of 1910, the opportunity came for Phillips to make a large sum of money from one commission, enough so that he could marry and make the down payment on a house in New Rochelle. A woman's fashion house offered Coles the chance to illustrate its Spring catalog, but the series of thirty figures would be needed in sixty days. Coles had always spent three to five days painting each of his pictures, so the request was almost ridiculous for him or any other artist. But because of the short deadline and the increasing stature of the Phillips name, the offer was so considerable that he could not afford to turn it down. The sum was more than he would make in a year as an artist for *Life*, and if he survived the two months of drudgery, he would have everything he wanted.

The sixty days were ones of grueling work. Coles seldom moved from his easel, slept but a few hours each night, and ate his meals while painting. He pushed himself to exhaustion. Time would prove that the work had taken a bad toll on his health.

Coles and Teresa were married in the Spring of 1910 and moved into a house at 158 Sutton Manor in New Rochelle. The town described by George M. Cohan as "Forty-Five Minutes from Broadway" was the home of America's top illustrators in the first quarter of the century. There was an anecdote — only a slight exaggeration — that the major magazines of the day were illustrated 90 percent by New Rochelle artists. Living and working there were Edward Penfield, the Leyendecker brothers, Orson Lowell, Walter Beach Humphrey, Leon Schaefer, and Norman Rockwell, among others. Coles Phillips left his Manhattan studio to work out of his home. The comfortable house on Sutton Manor had space for a large studio over the garage, which overlooked Long Island Sound.

Coles' studio was his office, and he was a most serious businessman. Painting did not come easy for him, and he often agonized over a picture, finding it necessary to do several versions before he was satisfied. Every artist has difficult periods, but Coles seemed to feel them more often and more acutely than most. Despite his seeming self-assurance, these arid periods were particularly tortuous for him and for Tess. He had less confidence in his abilities than he let on to any of his friends or fellow artists. Perhaps study and a stronger background in art would have helped him through the bleak periods, but even the most highly trained and talented artists know them.

Teresa recalled: "There were days when Cy could not draw, when he seemed to lose his touch. He worked through these spells, but it often meant beginning a painting all over again after several days, usually from a different model in order to get a fresh start.

"Those were terribly depressing times — particularly suicidal if the drawing was scheduled, if there was a magazine closing date staring him in the face and the painting had to go out as it was and there was no time to start a new one."

The artist set a regular nine-to-five workday for himself, but he would work evenings and weekends if necessary. The Kenyon College *Collegian*, the school's newspaper, ran a profile of its most famous alumnus that included a description of the artist and his work:

"Slim, blonde, blue-eyed, distinctly clean-cut, he does suggest his work. But it ends there. Although the woods are full of artists of a sort who bask in the warm admiration of feminine circles, Coles Phillips is not one of these. He's thoroughly a man's man, hates chatter, avoids functions like the plague and dislikes the type of artist who turns his studio into a drawing room. First of all, Coles Phillips is an artist. He is in addition a terrific worker and a business man. His big, airy studio in New Rochelle is his office. You can see him there by appointment for a few minutes if you want a magazine cover or an illustration — but not otherwise."

The artist's mornings were usually devoted to working with a model, the afternoons for developing the picture and preparing for the next morning's modeling session. Two or three days were needed to complete a picture once the modeling was finished. Like many of his contemporaries, Phillips refused to work from photographs or to use the pantograph, a mechanical tracing instrument. He always used live models and authentic props.

There was a good deal of glamour in being a "Phillips Girl" model, but the morning's work for $5 (with lunch) was a difficult job. Most often Coles made a sketch of the pose he wanted before the model arrived, and he arranged her accordingly. However, if he had no particular idea in mind and the model was experienced, he might have her strike a number of poses until something inspired him. The fade-away design might suggest that he only needed to paint a model's head, hands, and legs as the figure was essentially a flat design. But this was not the case. Since the absence of a definite figure outline had to be suggested by outside elements, painting the main portion of the body was just as difficult as if he had had to paint it realistically.

Phillips chose always to paint on a large surface, although his pictures were reduced to 9″ × 12″ or, for *Life* covers, 8″ × 10½″. The habit of painting larger — usually twice the size needed — was customary for an oil painter, but not for most watercolorists.

ONCE PHILLIPS left the advertising business to work for *Life*, it was several years before he returned to product advertising. It is difficult to imagine that Coles was not offered commissions for ad work. Perhaps he preferred not to do pictures for advertising once he achieved fame as an illustrator of books and magazines. But it was this very success that put him in demand as a creator of advertising art. The first company for which Phillips illustrated advertisements was Oneida Silversmiths. At the end of 1911 Coles' first fade-away appeared; Maxfield Parrish, Jon Witcomb, and J.C. Leyendecker also did pictures for Oneida at about the same

Coles Phillips painting a picture for Oneida Community Silversmiths in his Beaux Arts Building studio, 1924. Photo Carole Schau.

time. Oneida was the one company for which Coles produced pictures throughout his career.

With the growing popularity of the "Phillips Girl," both fade-away and full-figure, companies making products appealing to women used Phillips' pictures to sell their wares. Coles was especially adept at painting the texture of fabric, but even more skilled at showing the fabrics clinging to the female form. Holeproof Hosiery in Milwaukee gave him a contract, paying $50,000 over an extended period, to paint beautiful young women modeling the company's lingerie. The results were so striking that Luxite Hosiery Company called on him for similar pictures. In an era when there was mystery about sex, when it was not so accessible, the Coles Phillips women were sensational.

It is more than word play to say that advertisements are signs of the times, and there were occasions when an advertiser thought the artist had painted his women a bit overexposed. In 1924 the Norwich Pharmacal Company paid Phillips $6,000 to create a "Miss Sunburn" figure to sell its sunburn ointment. Coles painted a curvaceous beauty in a swimsuit, which delighted the company executives. The ad would be run first in the *The Saturday Evening Post* and subsequently in other national magazines.

Word came from the *The Post* art director that "Miss Sunburn" was sporting too much leg for decency. Since the picture was painted in watercolor, overlays had to be made to extend the bathing costume. The picture as it appeared to the public is shown on page 32. The difference can be noted by comparing this with the work on page 111, the picture as Coles painted it.

Despite the few inches less leg on display, "Miss Sunburn" was one of the most effective ads of the year. Not only was there a record increase in sales of the ointment, but salesmen reported "Miss Sunburn" placards were pilfered by the thousands from drugstore windows. This was remedied by printing small postcard-size pictures of the bathing beauty to be distributed at drug counters; the first printing and several more disappeared. Eventually, by the end of the year, "Miss Sunburn" appeared in a dozen magazines, on billboards, and on thousands of car windshields as window stickers.

In other instances, Phillips produced beautiful nudes to represent products in advertisements. For example, in 1920 the Clark Equipment Company, a Michigan-based manufacturer of truck parts, commissioned twelve leading artists to participate in a competition by painting their interpretations of "The Spirit of Transportation." Among the entrants were Phillips, Maxfield Parrish, Frank Leyendecker, Alphonse Mucha, and James Cady

In 1924 Phillips created this "Miss Sunburn" bathing beauty for the Norwich Pharmacal Company. *The Saturday Evening Post*'s art director considered the woman's suit as Phillips painted it (page 111) to be too revealing for its pages. Phillips extended the suit, and this is the final version as the public saw it. Courtesy Norwich Pharmacal Company.

Ewell. Coles submitted a winged, torch-bearing nude (page 102). Although the Parrish entry won the contest, the Phillips nude appeared nationally. The fact that a nude could be used in 1920 to sell an industrial product is a comment on the taste of the times and the talent of the artist.

IN 1911, COLES AND TESS hoped to enjoy the rewards of his huge success by taking a delayed honeymoon in Europe. There would be time for Coles to stop in Paris long enough to study at one of the academies. He also planned a stay in Munich where he would visit the German poster designer Ludwig Hohlwein. Like Phillips, Hohlwein was exclusively a watercolorist, and Coles looked forward to meeting the artist whom he admired.

But the trip was postponed, due mainly to the advice of John Ames Mitchell. The editor, who was by now a close family friend, told the artist that the additional training, especially in Paris, was unnecessary. What Phillips lacked in formal instruction, he made up, Mitchell said, with natural brilliance of design and imagination. He convinced Coles that his fresh viewpoint might be lost if he took too much time from his work. On an even more practical note, Mitchell reminded Coles that his art and name were just beginning to be accepted in America. To disappear at this time would be harmful to the development of that reputation.

Mitchell was a generous man, and his advice was surely not motivated by a fear of losing a first-rate cover artist. Whether or not he was correct in his advice about additional art training, he was on target about the artist's reputation. As early as 1910, Coles ranked with the best of the day's illustrators. *The New York Times* February 13, 1910, photogravure section ran a picture layout entitled "New York's Top Illustrators in Their Studios" in which, less than three years after his first drawing appeared, Phillips was pictured alongside Flagg, Leyendecker, and Harrison Fisher.

Beginning in 1911, Coles got offers to design covers for *Woman's Home Companion, Ladies' Home Journal,* and *McCall's. Good Housekeeping* signed Coles to do its monthly cover for five years, for a total of sixty covers. The remuneration and exposure via that magazine alone were unprecedented: What other periodical used the same cover artist every issue for five years?

For the first two years of the contract, *Good Housekeeping* carried Phillips' covers exclusively, all fade-away designs. The first was July 1912 (page 135). Sales for the magazine increased impressively during the period, but

Coles was beginning to regret having commited himself to the magazine. It was impossible, he was finding, to come up with a fresh idea for the same magazine month after month. The artist explained the situation to the editors, and they agreed to stretch the contract beyond five years. The remainder of the sixty alternated with covers by other artists.

In the years during and just after World War I, Phillips designed covers for *Liberty* and *Collier's*. His first of eleven covers for *The Saturday Evening Post* appeared in 1920.

TO KNOW SUCCESS as an illustrator during this era meant the opportunity to live well, and Coles and Tess were very comfortable in their large home. Unlike many illustrators who enjoyed flamboyant lifestyles, the Phillips family lived quietly. When plans for travel were put aside and Coles was firmly commited to many projects, he and Tess decided to start a family. In 1912 a son Clarence Coles, Jr., was born, followed in 1913 by John Hyde. In 1915 another son, Hyde, and in 1916 their only daughter, Joan, were born.

Coles decided to invest much of his newly earned wealth in real estate in New Rochelle, some of it in land adjacent to the reservoir and Wykagyl Country Club. On this property he began to raise pigeons, a pastime that had fascinated him since childhood. On his eighth birthday his mother asked what he wanted for a gift. He reported that a schoolmate had three pigeons for sale. The friend's father refused to let the boy keep the birds so they were available at 10 cents each. When Coles persuaded the family gardener to help him build a cote, his parents allowed him to have the birds.

As a boy Coles kept the pigeons as pets, but in his teen years he bred them for racing. When he went away to Kenyon, he had to sell the birds. Now that he was settled in New Rochelle and had property just minutes from his house, he decided to pursue the hobby again. At first he bred racers, but with the outbreak of World War I, the government needed homing pigeons for communication on the European front and Coles responded.

At America's entrance into the war Coles was thirty-seven. His health was precarious so he did not enlist for active service. But he did do a few war posters for the U.S. Fuel Administration (page 74), and the government found his birds invaluable in the war effort.

My Homing Pigeons–Birds of War

From a Painting
By
CÓLES PHILLIPS

Raising pigeons for war service is the unusual and very practical way in which Coles Phillips expresses his patriotism

PIGEONS *interest me more than anything else in the world. Ever since I was a small boy in Springfield, Ohio, I have had them for pets,"* says Coles Phillips, *"and now I am raising them for our soldiers. The Government has asked for thousands of birds, for, when other lines of communication are destroyed, pigeons released from the front line trenches fly back to the base with their messages, on which victory or defeat may hang. Ninety-seven per cent of messages entrusted to pigeons reach their destination."*

THAT *our readers may know some of Mr. Phillips's birds, the Government's new war heroes, he has shown in this picture a section of his own Homing Pigeon loft, where each pair of birds has its separate apartment, painted alternately black and white. The pigeons are beautiful in color and line, alert, strong, tight-feathered athletes—not the soft dove of fiction, but game birds with far-seeing eyes and courage unbelievable.*

During World War I Phillips raised homing pigeons for communications on the European front. This picture appeared in 1917 in the *Woman's Home Companion.* Photo Carole Schau.

Coles expanded the farm, and by 1921, in partnership with his friend James Montague, he opened the Silver Ring Squab Farm. Row upon row of pigeon lofts were built and some 4,500 birds kept. By 1927, the year of his death, Phillips and his partner were shipping 30,000 squab each year. Phillips explained to the New Rochelle *Standard-Star* in 1925: "Squabs have always been a hobby of mine. Men in my particular line of work ought to have an outside interest, but a hobby can also show a profit. I can't see gentlemen farmers who don't care whether their farms make money or not."

By the war years Phillips had reached the height of his popularity. He was accepting commissions for work one year in advance and needed a secretary to keep his work schedule and correspondence in order. Phillips enjoyed his celebrity status to a degree, but accepted it modestly. He would grant interviews if time allowed, and he enjoyed answering letters from

Coles with his three sons in 1919: (from left) Hyde, John, and Coles, Jr. Photo Carole Schau.

would-be illustrators. Although he was not a prima donna, he felt there was limited time for public appearances.

Because of the fame of his beautiful women, Coles was called on as an authority on feminine beauty, particularly to judge bathing beauty contests. Phillips always declined such invitations, but he did judge in absentia the Kenyon College annual Homecoming Queen. For many years Coles selected his alma mater's queen from photographs of the entrants mailed to his New Rochelle office.

While his success allowed Phillips to ask clients to call on him for all commission conferences, it also became clear that a New York City studio would be more convenient. Aside from the opportunity to work nearer to his clients, Coles admitted to Tess that he missed the stimulation of working in the city and meeting with other artists. When his friend J.C. Leyendecker recommended the Beaux Arts Building, on 40th Street across from Bryant Park, where he had kept a studio for many years, Coles decided to open an office there.

The years following the war were productive ones for Phillips. He did not turn out as many advertisements or covers as he had in the beginning — he did not need to — but the ones that he did were the best of his career.

EARLY IN 1924, Coles developed a kidney disease, diagnosed as tuberculosis of the kidneys for which surgery was required. The operation was successful, but relief was temporary. In the next three years Coles saw two dozen specialists in New York, Florida, and Europe to revive his failing health. Naturally these attempts cut drastically into the time when he usually painted. But the periods of required rest gave the artist time to evaluate his work of the past two decades. He told Tess that when he was well enough to paint again, he would start a new phase of his career.

After his death Teresa confirmed her husband's plans: "By the time he was forced definitely to give up to that illness and the agony that it entailed, he knew that he was going to do something different when he was better. He felt he had only just begun, and those who knew him best felt this too. He had definitely finished with drawing pretty girls, had carried that period to its logical conclusion. It was as though Book 1 of his career was finished and Book 2 was not yet begun. He had made his name known to the magazine public, but satisfying as that was for the time, it was only a phase, an apprenticeship." Whether Phillips planned to try his hand at "serious" work is not clear. It seems probable, though, that he would not have strayed from illustration.

Tess and Coles spent most of the year 1925–1926 in Switzerland, Italy, and France, staying longest in Switzerland where Coles took actinic ray treatments, a euphemism for "sunshine and rest." Since he was forced to do nothing but rest, he could only sketch views from his hotel. There was no opportunity for work. But he had no interest in sketching the European beauties to wile away the time. He had come to the conclusion that the charm of European women was overrated; the truly beautiful women of the world were in America.

He was restless to return to New York and to work, particularly since he hoped to launch a new phase of his career. "This is all perfect rot," he wrote to his sister Helen from Switzerland. "I am supposed to lie in the sun, but there is no sun. A good sunlamp in New Rochelle would do better."

FOREMOST ON HIS MIND when he and Tess returned to America was a joint project. They would collaborate on short stories that she would write and he would illustrate. Teresa had tried writing for her own amusement, but Coles was impressed with her talent and encouraged her to write professionally. Teresa brushed aside the urgings as flattery, but when Coles gave her a typewriter for her birthday in 1922, she began working in earnest. When two stories were completed, she showed them to the writer John Taintor Foote, a family friend. He encouraged her to submit one of them to *The Saturday Evening Post*. She agreed to do it, but under the name Teresa Hyde, so that she would not be published because of her husband's name. *The Post* fiction editor Thomas Costain (now known for his historic novels) returned the story, saying it was well written, but the plot was too thin. In a burst of courage she sent him the other story. Costain replied that it was acceptable for *The Post* and offered her $600 for it. "The Girl Who Would Be Queen" ran in a February 1923 issue of *The Post*.

Teresa's stories were romances, and she followed the rule "write about what you know." Her *Collier's* story "Phyllis the Unwanted," serialized in 1928, had as its central character an artist's model in love with Neil Farragut, "a popular and gifted artist," who used the young woman's image in a series of paintings for advertisements.

In 1926 the city of New Rochelle issued a commemorative booklet to celebrate its 250th anniversary. Because the city was the home of some of America's most notable illustrators, they were asked to donate pictures to decorate the booklet. Among the contributors were Norman Rockwell, Orson Lowell, and Edward Penfield. J.C. Leyendecker did the cover design. Coles Phillips began this picture, "The Siren Call," in 1925, but he was unable to complete it because of his trip to Europe for medical treatment. Leyendecker was asked to finish the picture, but since he was not a watercolor artist, he declined. In the end the editors thought the picture fine enough to publish unfinished. Photo Carole Schau.

Her writing was interrupted by the trip to Europe in 1925, and when she returned, she resumed her nursing career, this time caring for her husband. But when his medical expenses mounted, Tess assisted by writing again. She rose at dawn each day to write until 9 A.M. when Coles awoke and needed attention.

Coles hoped to illustrate his wife's "Ladies Need Daughters," which appeared in the October 16, 1926, issue of *The Post*. But he was not well enough to complete the pictures. One of them was on the easel in his studio at the time of his death, the last picture on which he worked.

Coles spent much of the last year of his life in severe pain, which he tried to blot from his mind by painting and working, when possible, at the Silver Ring Squab Farm. However, in the first months of 1927, he started to lose his eyesight, which made it impossible for him to continue painting. If he could no longer paint, he decided, he would try writing. He ordered stacks of yellow legal-size pads and began to write. Coles finished a long article on raising pigeons for *The Saturday Evening Post* and began a mystery novel, completing 40,000 words of it. He hoped, once recovered, to publish the novel with his own illustrations.

The story on pigeons was published in *The Post* on June 11, 1927. In the closing paragraph Coles wrote: "While in Italy my farm was the only pleasant thing I had to think about, which I tried to make the doctors understand. I was too weak to make it forceful enough. Finally I got my back up. I had spent all the money I had on doctors and their ill advice and I had improved in reverse ratio. I was going back to my farm and get well there without any doctor whatever."

On Monday, June 13, just two days after *The Post* article came out with its optimistic prediction, Coles Phillips died. J.C. Leyendecker had taken the four Phillips children into Manhattan that day to see the Fifth Avenue parade welcoming the young hero Charles Lindbergh back from France. At the funeral Leyendecker eulogized his friend as an artist "unique in his field, one with a highly developed sense of decoration and color . . . he was ahead of most men in depicting the American type of young womanhood."

COLES PHILLIPS had achieved enormous success in his chosen field in a short career, and his pictures were instantly identified by the public. But the question inevitably arises: Was he satisfied to be a painter of pretty women? Each picture is striking and engaging, and he seldom

The 1921 portrait of Coles Phillips painted by his friend, Norman Rockwell. Photo Carole Schau.

repeated a design, but was it enough to be the day's foremost painter of beautiful women?

It is not certain what ambitions Phillips had for himself, especially in light of his shortened productivity. He claimed, near the end, to want to move on to other subjects. If he wanted to do other things he was certainly caught in a difficult circle: the more beautiful women he created, the more demand there was for them. Editors usually refused anything but "girl pictures" from him, yet one would think the stature of the artist had developed enough — even though his reputation was based on his drawings of women — for him to demand a chance to create other types of pictures. After Coles' death Teresa reported that he was "sick of doing women pictures" and that he often did work on other subjects. "Cy loved to draw animals, but if he did anything but a girl, the editors called his efforts striking or interesting, but the conversation ended uniformly in one way: 'But, of course, what we want from you this time, Mr. Phillips, is one of your charming girls.'"

Yet the subject of a picture seemed less important to Phillips than its design. Portraiture and landscape, he admitted, held little appeal for him

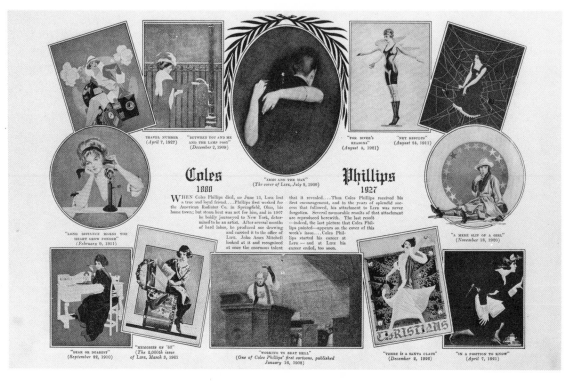

When Coles Phillips died in 1927, *Life* magazine ran this double-page tribute to one of its most popular cover artists. Phillips' first picture and his last were painted for *Life*.

as subjects; he could always fashion the human body into interesting patterns. Certainly design is the most striking aspect of a Phillips picture. He created precise, objective designs with sharp, graphic impact. Often the path created by space and color catch the eye before the beautiful face or the overall picture.

Teresa attested to Coles' fascination with design: "I can see him lean back from his easel, the smoke from a cigarette making him squint his eyes, criticizing everything he had just done, but saying, perhaps, while he pointed with his thumb to a certain spot, 'It's rather nice in there.' The 'in there' that he meant would invariably be some little space in the picture that no one but a draftsman would ever notice; one of those shapes of background that peep through, for instance, between the elbow and the head that is resting on the hand, the shapes that painters call voids. His arrangements of the masses, small and large, were to him much more exciting than the color or the idea, or whether the girl was pretty. Pure design, in other words, was his real love, and the fact that he made his reputation as a painter of pretty girls was more an accident than anything else."

MANY OF PHILLIPS later designs, both fade-away and full-dimensional, can be linked to an interest in Art Deco. The years during which Art Deco thrived in America, 1910–1930, coincide with the years of Phillips' artistic career. Art Deco was a reaction against the exaggerated curves, asymmetry, and decadent sensibilities of Art Nouveau. In its development, the style evolved in two separate directions. The French produced a decorative art that was graceful and curvilinear, which dominated for a time. Then younger craftsmen and designers, mainly in Germany, Holland, and Austria, adapted a form of Art Deco that was simpler, rectilinear, even austere. Phillips incorporated both types, from time to time, into his pictures. An example of each type can be seen in two advertisements created in 1924, both for Pratt & Lambert (pages 116–117). The one on page 116 employs the earlier style, and the one on page 117 the later rectilinear style. They express a unique variety in Art Deco design, considering Phillips did them the same year and for the same product. Because Phillips was one of the foremost American illustrators to make use of the techniques, he helped to popularize Art Deco in America.

His originality was obviously in design, not in the type of women he painted. His portrayal of women was within the accepted view of the day.

Undoubtedly the artist liked women, but he created no particular types, did not editorialize, or attempt to set standards. It was clearly a case of art imitating life. Phillips' art continued to be popular year after year because his view changed as women, their attitudes, and attitudes toward them altered. Some "girl artists" enjoyed a temporary popularity because they invented their own image of women, painting them as they seldom were and were not meant to be. But time and taste quickly bypassed these artists. Phillips' pictures of women may have been idealized, but he faithfully mirrored the women he and all America knew.

If Coles Phillips unintentionally chronicled the women of an era, the two decades 1907–1927 could not have witnessed a more dramatic change for him to record. The years represent the passing of only one generation, but one in which there was striking change. Phillips' first pictures were painted during the Edwardian Era, the last in the midst of Prohibition. To view Phillips' early and late magazine covers side by side makes the differences immediately apparent. The typical theme of the early covers, mainly for *Life*, is a satire on the elegant strategist, whose main occupation is capturing a husband, preferably a rich one. In sharp contrast, the later Phillips' woman of the mid-1920s is interestingly independent. She may lack the "sweetness" of the coyly scheming beauties of two decades earlier, but she is more experienced, bolder, brighter, obviously sexual.

Each extreme has her charm. But it is the development of the American woman in the hundreds of pictures created by Coles Phillips that is of particular interest in our time. Obviously during Coles Phillips' 20-year career, the "All-American Girl" grew up.

Chronology

Coles Phillips, 1880–1927

October 1880. Born in Springfield, Ohio. Named Clarence Coles Phillips, third child of Jason W. and Anna Size Phillips.

1897. First published illustrations for *The American,* a weekly magazine published in Springfield.

1900. Began work for American Radiator Company, Springfield.

September 1901. Entered Kenyon College at Gambier, Ohio, class of 1905.

June 1904. Left Ohio for New York City. Worked for eastern office of American Radiator Company.

1905. Studied at the Chase School of Art and the Free School, New York. First art job as staff artist for an advertising agency.

1906. Opened C.C. Phillips & Company Agency, his own advertising agency.

January 1907. Closed the C.C. Phillips Company.

February 1907. Opened a studio at 13 West 29th Street to work as a freelance artist.

March 1907. First cartoon sold to *Life* magazine, establishing a relationship with the magazine that lasted twenty years.

April 1907. First *Life* cartoon published.

December 1907. Met Teresa Hyde and became engaged the following month.

February 1908. First magazine cover published by *Life* magazine.

May 1908. First Phillips fade-away design appeared on the cover of *Life.*

1909. First book illustrations for *Michael Thwaites's Wife* by Miriam Michelson and *Cords of Vanity* by James Branch Cabell.

1910. Married Teresa Hyde and moved to Sutton Manor in New Rochelle, New York. Closed Manhattan studio and opened home office. Illustrated *The Fascinating Mrs. Halton* by E.F. Benson.

1911. *A Gallery of Girls by Coles Phillips* published by The Century Company. First magazine cover work for publications other than *Life* (*Woman's Home Companion, McCall's, Ladies' Home Journal*). Signed contract to do every *Good Housekeeping* cover for five years. Accepted first commissions to create advertising art for Oneida Community Silver.

1912. *A Young Man's Fancy*, collection of Phillips drawings published by Bobbs-Merrill. First son, Clarence Coles, Jr., born. (Died 1960.)

1913. Son John Hyde born. (Died 1974.)

1915. Son Hyde born. (Died 1952.)

1916. Daughter and last child, Joan, born.

1917. Did poster work for U.S. Fuel Administration. Raised carrier pigeons for U.S. government war effort in Europe.

1920. Entered Clark Equipment Company "The Spirit of Transportation" competition. First covers for *The Saturday Evening Post.*

1921. Established Silver Ring Squab Farm in New Rochelle.

1923. Illustrated Temple Bailey's *The Dim Lantern*. Teresa Phillips' first short story sold to *The Saturday Evening Post.*

1924. Illustrated Temple Bailey's *Peacock Feathers*. Created "Miss Sunburn" ad for Norwich Pharmacal Company. First surgery performed on Phillips for kidney ailment.

June 1925. Phillips sailed for Europe for medical treatment. Visited Italy, France, and Switzerland.

June 1926. Teresa and Coles returned from Europe. He accepted commissions again to paint.

January 1927. Phillips' sight began to fail and he gave up painting to write.

June 13, 1927. Died at home in New Rochelle, New York. Age 47. Cremated at Fresh Ponds, Long Island.

Illustrations

ALTHOUGH it was as a cover artist that Coles Phillips earned his reputation as one of America's most imaginative illustrators, his first art job was as a cartoon artist for the old *Life* magazine in 1907. His drawings, very much in the style of Charles Dana Gibson, usually appeared on the magazine's center double-page spread. They gave Phillips his first exposure and preceded his first cover work for *Life* by a year. At the height of his popularity Phillips worked almost exclusively creating magazine covers and pictures for advertisements, but he also found time to accept a few commissions to illustrate books, such as *Michael Thwaite's Wife* in 1909, *The Fascinating Mrs. Halton* in 1910, *The Dim Lantern* in 1923, and *Peacock Feathers* in 1924.

Illustrations for *The Reveille*, Kenyon College, 1901–1904. Photos Thomas B. Greenslade.

"Her Choice," cartoon for *Life* magazine, June 20, 1907. Photo Carole Schau.

"Prosperity," cartoon for *Life* magazine, September 26, 1907. Photo Carole Schau.

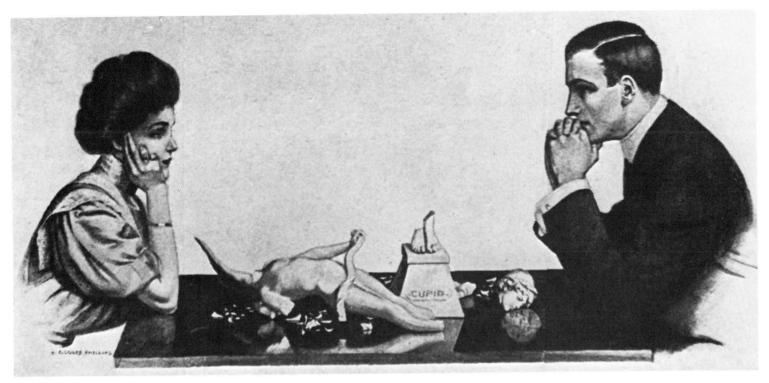

"Till Death Do Us Part," cartoon for *Life* magazine, 1908. Photo Carole Schau.

"Working to Beat Hell," cartoon for *Life* magazine, January 16, 1908. Photo Carole Schau.

"A Man After Her Own Heart," cartoon for *Life* magazine, February 20, 1908. Photo Carole Schau.

"Wise, Likewise, and Otherwise," cartoon for *Life* magazine, April 19, 1908. Photo Carole Schau.

"A Clerical Error," cartoon for *Life* magazine,
April 2, 1908. Photo Carole Schau.

"Mistress Mary," cartoon for *Life* magazine,
1908. Photo Carole Schau.

"Ashes of Yesterday," cartoon for *Life* magazine,
May 7, 1908. Photo Carole Schau.

"Jilted," cartoon for *Life* magazine,
May 7, 1908. Photo Carole Schau.

"Christmas Morning," cartoon for *Life* magazine, December 17, 1908. Photo Carole Schau.

"A Ball Gown," cartoon for *Life* magazine, 1909. Photo Carole Schau.

Illustrations for *Michael Thwaites' Wife* by Miriam Michelson. Published by Doubleday, Page & Company, 1909. Photos Carole Schau.

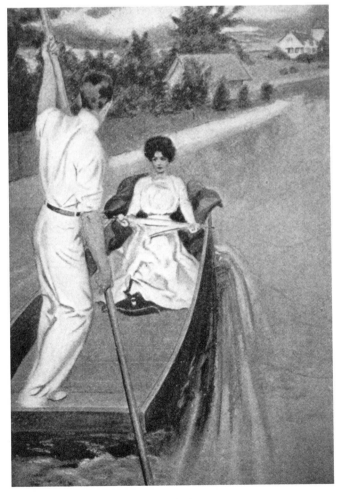

Illustrations for *The Fascinating Mrs. Halton* by E.F. Benson. Published by Grosset & Dunlap, 1910.

Frontispiece for *Cords of Vanity* by James Branch Cabell, 1909. Photo Carole Schau.

"The Midshipmite," 1912 Navy Girl. Painted for Brigade of Midshipmen, United States Naval Academy, 1912. Photo Carole Schau.

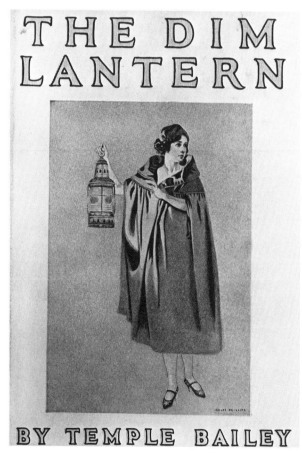

Cover for *The Dim Lantern* by Temple Bailey. Published by The Penn Publishing Company, 1923. Photo Carole Schau.

Frontispiece for *Peacock Feathers* by Temple Bailey. Published by The Penn Publishing Company, 1924. Photo Carole Schau.

Advertisements

BEFORE HE SOARED to prominence at *Life* magazine as an illustrator and cover artist, Coles Phillips worked in various facets of the advertising industry—as an artist, salesman, and owner of an agency. But throughout these early years, his goal was to become a painter. In 1907, he finally began to be recognized for his drawings of beautiful young women, and it was four years before Phillips could be lured back to advertising. But it was the very success of the "Phillips Girl" that made businessmen want Phillips pictures to represent their wares. His first advertising work was for Oneida Silversmiths, which was also the only company for which he did illustrations continuously during his twenty-year career. The Phillips woman sold such diverse products as cars, soap, and paint, but the most effective pictures for advertising were those for clothing. The illustrations for such companies as Holeproof Hosiery, Luxite Hosiery, and Jantzen made best use of Phillips' talent for painting full-figured, beautiful young women.

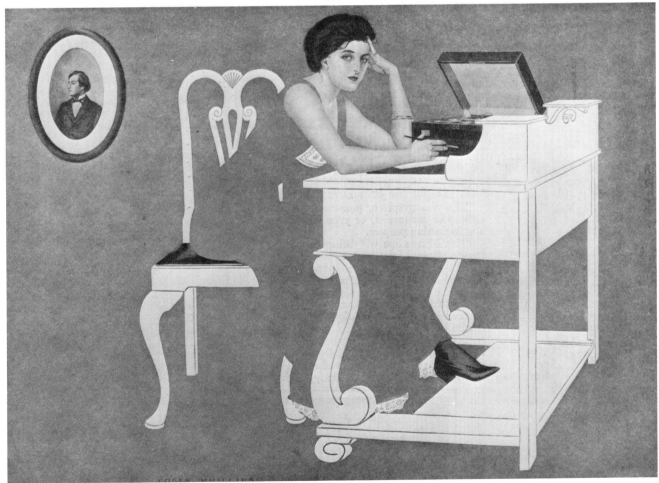

Oneida Community advertisements for Community Silver, Oneida Ltd. Silversmiths, 1911.

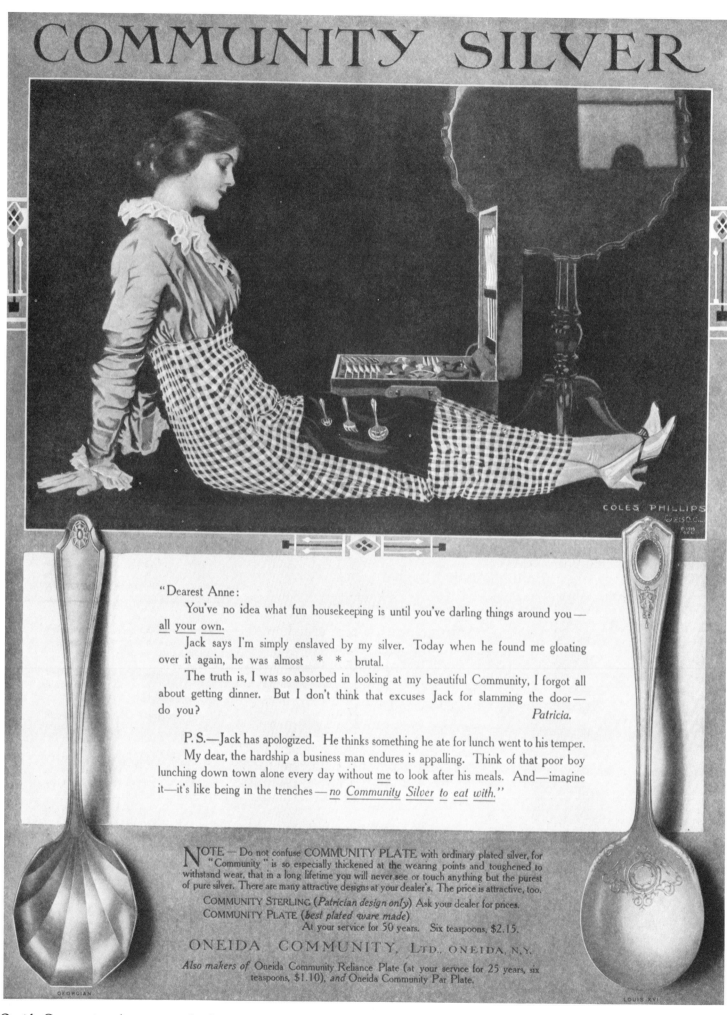

Oneida Community advertisement for Community Silver, Oneida Ltd. Silversmiths, 1915.

COMMUNITY SILVER

GEORGIAN   COLES PHILLIPS   SHERATON

DIARY OF A MERE MAN   *Thursday, ————— 11, 1913*

"FOUND Nan 'peeved' today. Cause—'hideous' spoons from Aunt Amelia. 'I've set my heart upon Community Silver,' Nan protested, 'and just *must* have some for my own!'   *   * I determined not to yield.

Friday, ————— 12, 1913

Dragged to the jeweler's by Nan *   * shown a Community Silver chest with the million-dollar-look. Thumbed the price tag—a hundred. Had the chest sent home. (Nan said a smaller one would do, but I insisted.)

Saturday, ————— 13, 1913

Party tonight. Table brilliant—Nan radiant."

BEST PLATED WARE MADE   AT YOUR DEALER'S
AT YOUR SERVICE FOR 50 YEARS   6 TEASPOONS, $2.15 (engraving extra); In Canada, $2.75

Oneida Community advertisement for Community Silver, Oneida Ltd. Silversmiths, 1915.

Willys-Overland Company advertisements, 1915. Photo Carole Schau.

AN AFTERNOON COSTUME BY MADAME JENNY

Designed Especially for the Woman's Home Companion

Copyright, 1915, by The Crowell Publishing Company

COLES PHILLIPS

Advertisement for dress design by Madame Jenny, 1915. Collection Mr. and Mrs. Joseph Suess. Photo Carole Schau.

George Frost Company advertisement, 1911. Collection Vincent Petragnani.

Spring is Here!

Apple-blossom time is here again.

Spring is just poking its welcome nose into our midst. The chill of winter is gone. The thrill of spring is here.

Millions of trees are studded with buds. Millions of brooks are merrily rippling and flowing along apace. Ice and snow are no more. Winter is done.

With it all comes the delight of being in the big outdoors.

Dear old Mother Nature is smilingly beckoning and begging you into the highways and byways of the peaceful, beneficial, wide-open country.

From now on every day is a motoring day.

Motoring is one of the real joys of living. Also, it's a necessity to those who value time, and wish to annihilate distance.

Get your Overland *now*.

Model 80 $1075
TOURING CAR

Model 81 Roadster . . $795
Model 80 Roadster . . . $1050
Six—Model 82 . . . . . $1475
7 Passenger Touring Car
Model 80 Coupé $1600
4 Passenger Coupé
All prices f. o. b. Toledo, Ohio.
Catalogue on request. Please address Department 200
"Made in U. S. A."

Model 81 $850
TOURING CAR

THE WILLYS-OVERLAND COMPANY, TOLEDO, OHIO

$1075
MODEL 80 TOURING CAR F.O.B. TOLEDO

COLES PHILLIPS

Willys-Overland Company advertisement, 1915.

Order Your Overland!

The new Overland is the most practical car for your whole family.

Also it's a beauty. Finished in that majestic dark Brewster green it is attractively stylish yet simple. The body design is artistic and graceful.

The long underslung rear springs make it ride with ease and perfect smoothness. You can drive all day without tiring.

That's one reason why the Overland is so popular with American women.

Here's another:

It is the simplest of cars to drive. On the steering column is a set of electric buttons. By just pressing these buttons the car is started, stopped and lighted.

Everything about the Overland is designed for comfort and convenience. It is distinctly a family car.

Our dealer has a new one for you. Spring is here. Order yours today.

Model 80 $1075
TOURING CAR

Model 81 Roadster . . . $795
Model 80 Roadster . . . $1050
Six—Model 82 . . . . . $1475
7 Passenger Touring Car
Model 80 Coupé $1600
4 Passenger Coupé
All prices f. o. b. Toledo, Ohio.

Model 81 $850
TOURING CAR

Catalogue on request. Please address Department 200
"Made in U.S.A."
THE WILLYS-OVERLAND COMPANY, TOLEDO, OHIO

$1050
MODEL 80 ROADSTER F.O.B. TOLEDO

Willys-Overland Company advertisement, 1916.

SIX *Overland* $1145

COLES PHILLIPS

A Timely and Fitting Suggestion

Christmas is only a few days away. Once again the annual eternal question of "what to give" stares you in the face. You desperately think of this, that and the other thing, yet you can decide on nothing that will particularly please the whole family.

You do not want to give the average expected gift. On the contrary you are only too anxious to do something entirely out of the ordinary — if you could but think of it.

So here's a thought. Give them a fine, big, useful and beautiful Overland Six! Present it yourself Christmas morning. Don't tell a soul. Just drive up to the house on the quiet; call them all out; point to the dandy new Overland and say—"It's yours!" Then watch their loving faces light up with joy and delight. It will without question be the best Christmas, by far, of their entire life.

Catalogue on request

The Overland Six is large enough to seat seven comfortably; powerful enough to take you any place; fitted with every convenience which makes driving, for your wife and daughter, simple and easy. It is handsomely proportioned, gracefully designed and luxuriously upholstered. It's the car of cars. Its cost, value considered, is exceedingly moderate. Orders placed now can be delivered Christmas morning — right at your front door.

Consider what an endless chain of pleasure, an Overland Six will provide year in and out for the whole family.

Also there is the Model 83 — 5 passenger touring car — $750; the Model 75 — 5 passenger touring car — $615; roadsters $725 and $595 — all f. o. b. Toledo.

Make arrangements with the Overland dealer today.

The Willys-Overland Company, Toledo, Ohio

Willys-Overland Company advertisement, 1916. Collection Mr. and Mrs. Joseph Suess.

Luxite Hosiery Company advertisement, 1917.

PROPER Shampooing is what makes your hair beautiful. It brings out all the real life, lustre, natural wave and color, and makes it soft, fresh and luxuriant.

Your hair simply needs frequent and regular washing to keep it beautiful, but it cannot stand the harsh effect of ordinary soap. The free alkali, in ordinary soaps, soon dries the scalp, makes the hair brittle, and ruins it. This is why discriminating women use

WATKINS
MULSIFIED COCOANUT OIL
FOR
SHAMPOOING

This clear, pure, and entirely greaseless product, cannot possibly injure, and does not dry the scalp or make the hair brittle, no matter how often you use it.

Two or three teaspoonfuls will cleanse the hair and scalp thoroughly. Simply moisten the hair with water and rub it in. It makes an abundance of rich, creamy lather, which rinses out easily, removing every particle of dust, dirt, dandruff and excess oil.

The hair dries quickly and evenly, and has the appearance of being much thicker and heavier than it is. It leaves the scalp soft and the hair fine and silky, bright, fresh-looking and fluffy, wavy and easy to do up.

You can get MULSIFIED COCOANUT OIL at any drug store, and a 50-cent bottle should last for months. Splendid for children.

If your druggist does not have it, an original bottle will be mailed direct upon receipt of price

THE R. L. WATKINS CO., Dept. F CLEVELAND, OHIO

R.L. Watkins Company advertisement, 1917.

Poster for U.S. Fuel Administration, 1917. Courtesy The Library of Congress.

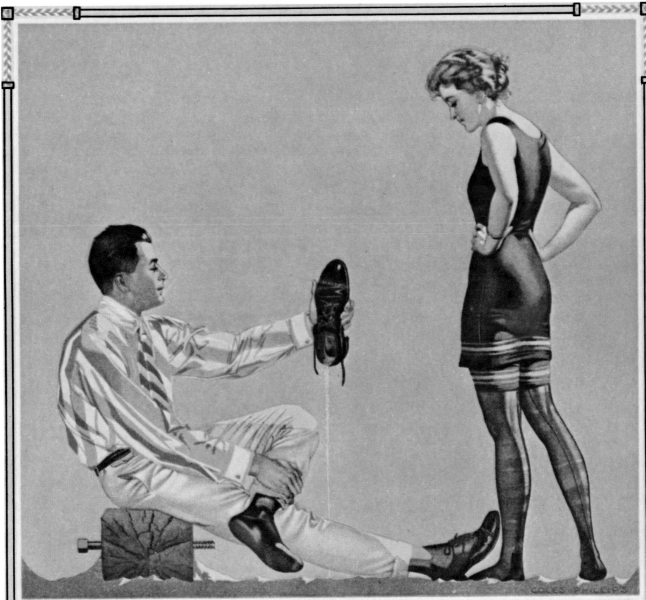

©L.T. Inc.

Hose of Luxite

For Men, Women and Children

HOSIERY, today, is regarded more important to the charm of personal appearance than ever before. Look your best—not on state occasions only—but *always*; that is the modern idea.

Hose of Luxite have the spirit of Luxury—yet they are not extravagant. Shapely, shimmering and closely-woven—the product of beautiful materials, pure dyes and specialized methods. Long wear and elegance are combined in inseparable union.

In Japanese Pure Silk: Men's, 50c per pair; Women's, $1.00, $1.10 and $1.50.

Other styles in Gold-Ray (scientific silk), lisle and cotton. Prices as low as 25c per pair, for Men, Women and Children.

Ask your dealer to supply you. If he cannot do so, write for price list and descriptive booklet today.

LUXITE TEXTILES, Inc., 611 Fowler Street, MILWAUKEE, WIS.

Makers of High-Grade Hosiery Since 1875

New York   Chicago   San Francisco   Liverpool

A beautiful color print of the above painting by Coles Phillips, size 12x11 inches, will be sent upon receipt of 15 cents in stamps.

Luxite Hosiery Company advertisement, 1917.

Willys-Overland Company advertisement, 1917. Courtesy Jane and Stephen Klain.

Oneida Community advertisement for Community Plate, Oneida Ltd. Silversmiths, 1917.

Painted by Coles Phillips for Luxite Textiles, Inc.

© L. T. Inc.

Hose as Shapely as the Curves of the Figure

THE translucent shimmer of Luxite Hosiery half reveals and half conceals. Its texture is so wonderfully soft and silken you can draw a Luxite silk stocking through your finger ring. Luxite launders beautifully because these hose contain no adulterations whatever—nothing but super-fine materials and pure dyes. Naturally Luxite Hosiery wears long and always looks beautiful.

Women's Silk Faced, $1.10; Pure Thread Japanese Silk, $1.30 to $2.25. Other styles 55c upward.
Men's Silk Faced, 65c; Pure Thread Japanese Silk, 85c and $1.10. Other styles 35c up. Children's, 55c up.

LUXITE TEXTILES, Inc., 654 Fowler Street, Milwaukee, Wisconsin

New York   Chicago   San Francisco   *Makers of High Grade Hosiery Since 1875*   Liverpool, England   Sydney, Australia
LUXITE TEXTILES OF CANADA, Limited, London, Ont.   (984)

COLES PHILLIPS

Luxite Hosiery Company advertisement, 1919.

SCRANTON

The Welcoming Window

Welcome gleams from a window that is gracefully curtained. The charm of a house seen from without, and the atmosphere of each room within, depend largely upon the draping of the windows. The lovely Scranton lace curtains, including Maid-O-Nets with lace edges, and filet nets, lend distinction to any room in any house. They are not expensive.

Send for our free booklet "New Outlooks for Every Home" showing the newest ideas for draping windows of all types, with beautiful illustrations and full details. If you have a difficult curtain problem, write to our Service Department about it. Without charge we will gladly send you our advice.

Ask your dealer to show you the new line of Scranton Overdraperies.

THE SCRANTON LACE COMPANY
SCRANTON, PA.

SCRANTON
FILET NETS AND LACE CURTAINS

Scranton Lace Company advertisement, 1919.

Willys-Overland Company advertisements, 1916. Photo Carole Schau.

Willys-Overland Company advertisement, 1915. Photo Carole Schau.

Willys-Overland Company advertisement, 1915. Photo Carole Schau.

Willys-Overland Company advertisement, 1916. Photos Carole Schau.

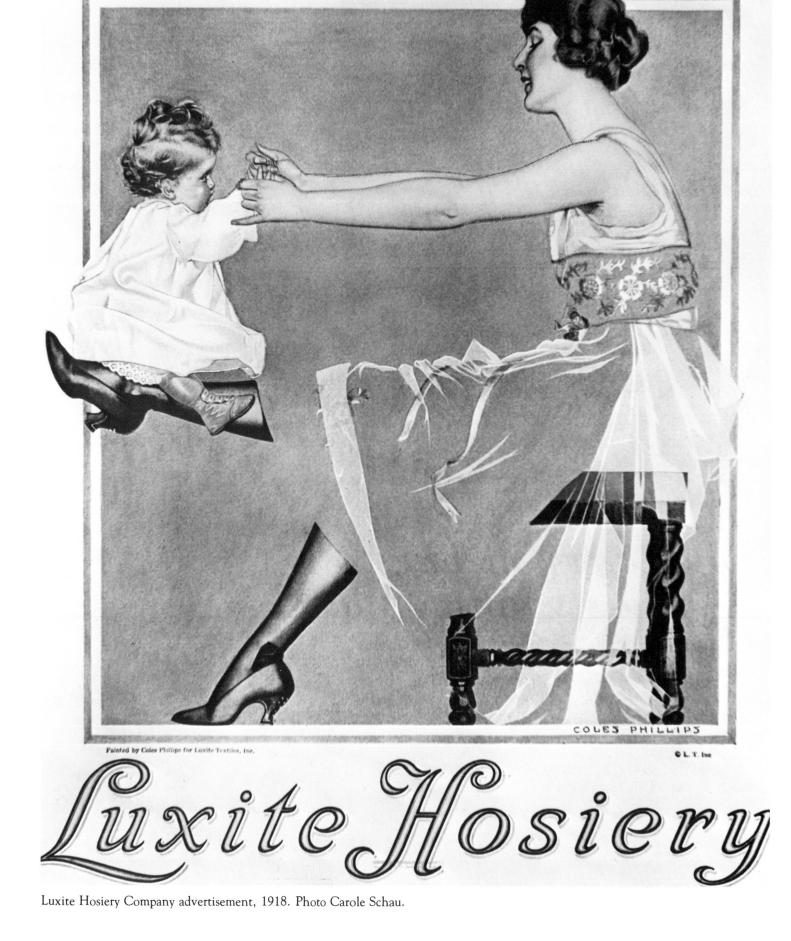

Painted by Coles Phillips for Luxite Textiles, Inc.

© L. T. Inc

COLES PHILLIPS

Luxite Hosiery

Luxite Hosiery Company advertisement, 1918. Photo Carole Schau.

Jell-O advertisement, 1919. Photo Carole Schau.

Western Company advertisement, 1919. Photo Carole Schau.

Palmolive Company advertisement for Palmolive Soap, 1920. Collection Mr. and Mrs. Joseph Suess. Photo Carole Schau.

America Chicle Company advertisement for Adams Gum, 1920. Photo Carole Schau.

Luxite Hosiery Company advertisement, 1920. Photo Carole Schau.

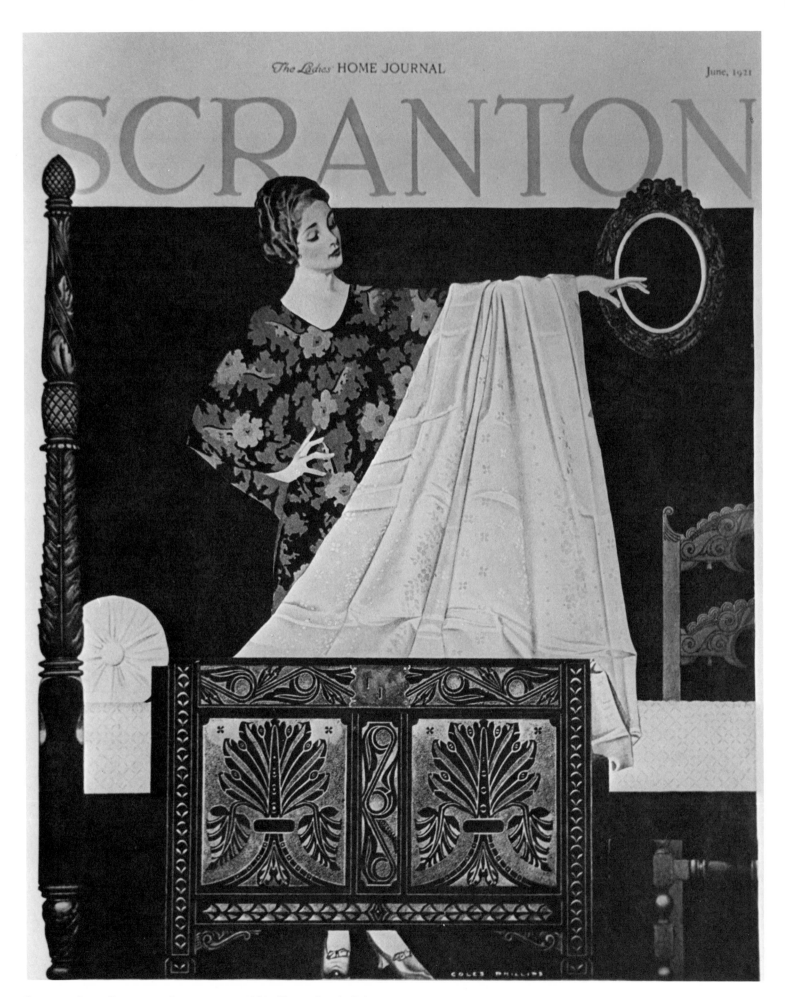

Scranton Lace Company advertisement, 1921. Photo Carole Schau.

Holeproof Hosiery Company advertisement, 1921. Collection Jane and Stephen Klain. Photo Carole Schau.

Jantzen Swimsuit Company advertisement, 1921. Courtesy The Jantzen Company. Photo Carole Schau.

Palmolive Company advertisement for Palmolive Soap, 1921. Photo Carole Schau.

Holeproof Hosiery Company advertisement, 1921. Photo Carole Schau.

IN any room in any house, it is the curtaining of the windows that lends the final touch of charm. There are lovely Scranton lace curtains, including our new Maid-O-Net designs with lace edges, also filet nets, at all prices.

Send for free booklet "New Outlooks for Every Home," showing the newest ideas for draping windows of all types, with beautiful illustrations and full details. If you have a difficult curtain problem, write to our Service Department about it. Without charge we will gladly send you our advice.

THE SCRANTON LACE CO., SCRANTON, PA.

Ask your dealer to show you also the beautiful new Scranton Embroideries.

SCRANTON
FILET NETS AND LACE CURTAINS

Scranton Lace Company advertisement, 1919.

Scranton Lace Company advertisement, 1919.

EYES besides yours are sure to admire your hosiery if it be this fairy-fine Luxite. Woven of the finest Japanese silk thread, and fitting every curve perfectly, Luxite is the silk hosiery supreme for both appearance and wear. Made for men, too, to emphasize "well groomed."

LUXITE TEXTILES, Inc., 673 Fowler Street, Milwaukee, Wisconsin
NEW YORK   CHICAGO   SAN FRANCISCO   SYDNEY, AUSTRALIA
Makers of High Grade Hosiery Since 1875   LUXITE TEXTILES OF CANADA, LIMITED, London, Ont.

Luxite Hosiery Company advertisement, 1919.

© H. H. Co.

COLES PHILLIPS

THE secret of trim lustrous ankles with many well-dressed women is not a matter of what they pay for their hose, but what kind they get. More and more, women are discovering that Holeproof Hosiery offers all the style, sheerness and lustrous beauty that fashion demands, in combination with a fine-spun strength that gives extraordinarily long service.

Leading stores are now showing the newest ideas in regular and fancy styles in Silk, Silk Faced, Silk and Wool, Wool Mixtures and Lisles, for men, women and children.

Holeproof Hosiery

HOLEPROOF HOSIERY COMPANY, Milwaukee, Wisconsin
Holeproof Hosiery Company of Canada, Limited, London, Ontario

Holeproof Hosiery Company advertisement, 1920. Collection Mr. and Mrs. Joseph Suess.

Scranton Lace Company advertisement, 1920. Collection Mr. and Mrs. Joseph Suess.

"The Spirit of Transportation" advertisement for Clark Equipment Company, 1920. Courtesy Clark Equipment Co.

George W. Blabon Company advertisement, 1920. Collection Mr. and Mrs. Joseph Suess.

Holeproof Hosiery Company advertisement, 1921.

National Lamp Company advertisement for National Mazda Lamps, 1921.

Biberman Brothers Company advertisement for L'Aiglon Dresses, 1921.

Fiberloid Corporation advertisement, 1922.

Holeproof Hosiery Company advertisement, 1922.

Holeproof Hosiery

HOLEPROOF offers women a sensible combination in hosiery that can be found in no other makes—long wear and beautiful appearance.

Some hose may equal Holeproof in appearance but they lack the phenomenal durability that has made Holeproof famous. Others may approach Holeproof in wearing quality, but at the sacrifice of fine texture and sheerness.

If you are interested in getting hosiery that will give extraordinary wear and at the same time is sheer and beautiful, ask for Holeproof.

At all good stores—in many styles, in all approved colors. Silk, silk-and-wool, wool, silk-faced, and lusterized lisle. Styles also for men and children. If not available locally, write for booklet and prices.

HOLEPROOF HOSIERY COMPANY, MILWAUKEE, WISCONSIN
Holeproof Hosiery Company of Canada, Limited, London, Ontario

© H. H. Co.

Holeproof Hosiery Company advertisement, 1922.

COMMUNITY PLATE

A Chest of Dreams and Silver

Oneida Community advertisement for Community Plate, Oneida Ltd. Silversmiths, 1924.

"Miss Sunburn" advertisement for Unguentine, 1924. Courtesy Norwich Pharmacal Company.

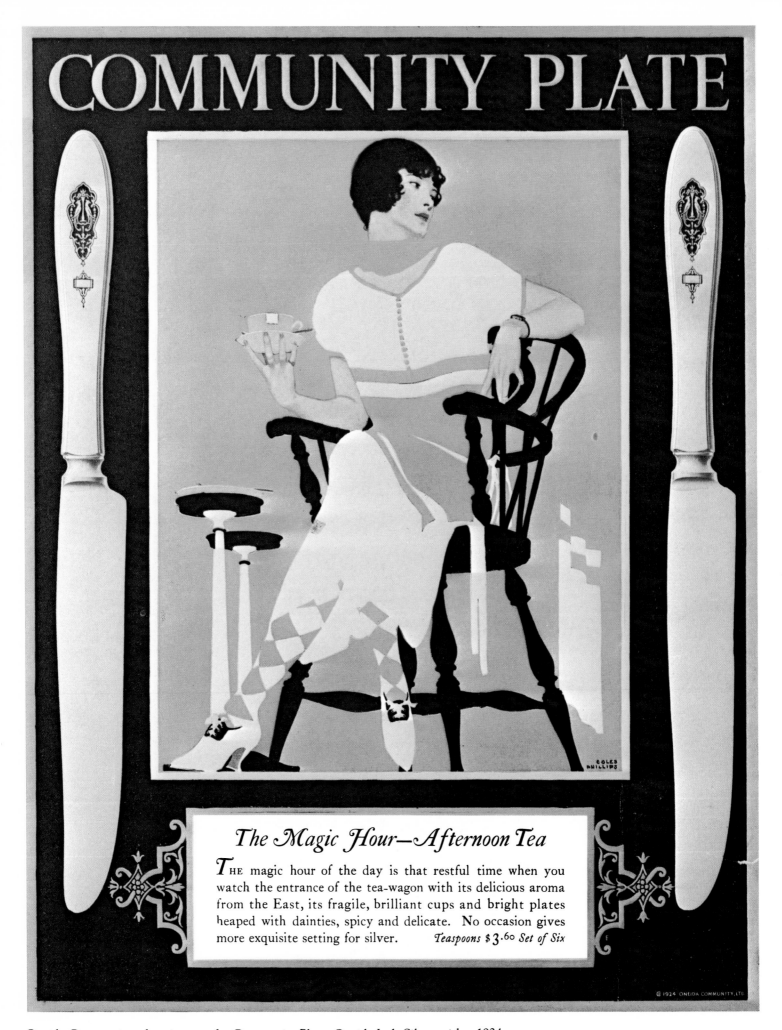

COMMUNITY PLATE

The Magic Hour—Afternoon Tea

THE magic hour of the day is that restful time when you watch the entrance of the tea-wagon with its delicious aroma from the East, its fragile, brilliant cups and bright plates heaped with dainties, spicy and delicate. No occasion gives more exquisite setting for silver. *Teaspoons* $3.60 *Set of Six*

Oneida Community advertisement for Community Plate, Oneida Ltd. Silversmiths, 1924.

Scranton Lace Company advertisement, 1922. Photo Carole Schau.

Give Her a L'Aiglon for Xmas

No. 2767—A smart, crisp frock of Imported Gingham trimmed with white pique. The collar boasts of a touch of hand embroidery. Blue, brown, black, green, lavender or tan. Packed in a Christmas box $7.00

Slightly higher West of the Rockies

Biberman Brothers, Inc. advertisement for L'Aiglon Dresses, 1922. Collection Mr. and Mrs. Joseph Suess. Photo Carole Schau.

Oneida Community advertisement for Community Plate, Oneida Ltd. Silversmiths, 1922.

Pratt & Lambert, Inc. advertisement for Vitralite Paints, 1924. Courtesy Pratt & Lambert, Inc. Photo Carole Schau.

Pratt & Lambert, Inc. advertisement for Vitralite Paints, 1924. Courtesy Pratt & Lambert, Inc. Photo Carole Schau.

COMMUNITY PLATE

Silverware of Quality

Oneida Community advertisement for Community Plate, Oneida Ltd. Silversmiths, 1924. Photo Carole Schau.

Magazine Covers

C OLES PHILLIPS' magazine covers catapulted him to early fame, and it was to this medium that he devoted most of his career. Although he was best known for his work at *Life* magazine, hundreds of Phillips pictures adorned many different magazines during his years of peak popularity. The first Coles Phillips magazine cover appeared in 1908 on *Life* magazine; his last was published posthumously by *Life* in 1927. It was also *Life* that carried the initial fade-away designs, the technique on which Phillips' fame rests. The fade-away designs met with enormous success, and the artist was called upon to create covers for such popular periodicals as *Good Housekeeping*, *Collier's*, *Liberty*, *McCall's*, and others. The covers give a clear picture not only of the artist's development, but of the changes in the American woman's image that took place in those twenty years.

"R.S.V.P.," *Life* magazine cover, March 12, 1908. Photo Carole Schau.

"Arms and the Man," *Life* magazine cover, July 8, 1909. Photo Carole Schau.

"The Time of Her Life," *Life* magazine cover, August 5, 1909. Photo Carole Schau.

"Dates," *Life* magazine cover, Suffragette Number, September 23, 1909. Photo Carole Schau.

"Divine Service," *Life* magazine cover, January 28, 1909. Photo Carole Schau.

"Her Move," *Life* magazine cover, Flirt's Number, June 10, 1909. Photo Carole Schau.

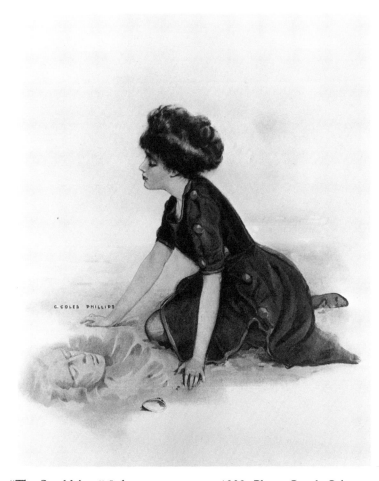

"The Sand Man," *Life* magazine cover, 1909. Photo Carole Schau.

"Know All Men by These Presents," *Life* magazine cover, January 27, 1910. Photo Carole Schau.

"From the Mirror," *Life* magazine cover, August 19, 1909. Photo Carole Schau.

"The Butterfly Chase," *Life* magazine cover, March 10, 1910. Photo Carole Schau.

Life magazine cover, Auto Number, January 6, 1910. Collection Jane and Stephen Klain. Photo Carole Schau.

"The House That Jack Built," *Life* magazine cover, March 31, 1910. Photo Carole Schau.

"Thoroughbreds," *Life* magazine cover, 1910. Photo Carole Schau.

"Reflections of a Bachelor," *Life* magazine cover, April 28, 1910. Photo Carole Schau.

"Discarding from Strength," *Life* magazine cover, May 12, 1910. Photo Carole Schau.

"Hoot Mon," *Life* magazine cover, October 20, 1910. Photo Carole Schau.

"A Present-Day Saint," *Life* magazine cover, December 22, 1910. Photo Carole Schau.

"Such Stuff as Dreams Are Made Of," *Life* magazine cover, 1910. Photo Carole Schau.

"Long Distance Lends Enchantment," *Life* magazine cover, February 9, 1911. Photo Carole Schau.

"Forward and Back," *Life* magazine cover, March 16, 1911. Photo Carole Schau.

"A Friend of the Family," *Life* magazine cover, Easter Number, April 6, 1911. Photo Carole Schau.

"Without Accompaniment," *Life* magazine cover, Summer Girl Number, June 15, 1911. Photo Carole Schau.

"A Call to Arms," *Life* magazine cover, July 27, 1911. Photo Carole Schau.

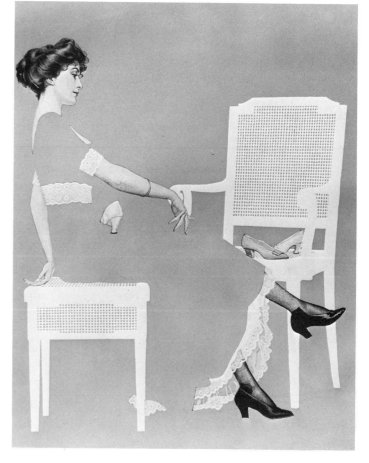

"The Survival of the Fittest," *Life* magazine cover, August 31, 1911. Photo Carole Schau.

Life magazine cover, Summer Fiction Number, September 14, 1911. Photo Carole Schau.

"The Light Housekeeper," *Life* magazine cover, October 12, 1911. Photo Carole Schau.

Good Housekeeping magazine cover, July 1912. Photo Carole Schau.

Life magazine cover, 1912. The pictures within the picture are previous Phillips *Life* covers. Photo Carole Schau.

"Class 1. Widows," *Life* magazine cover, Widow's Number, December 26, 1912. Photo Carole Schau.

Good Housekeeping magazine covers, 1912. Photos Carole Schau.

Good Housekeeping magazine cover, September 1913. Photo Carole Schau.

Good Housekeeping magazine covers, 1912–1913. Photos Carole Schau.

Good Housekeeping magazine cover, June 1914. Photo Carole Schau.

Good Housekeeping magazine covers, 1914. Photos Carole Schau.

Good Housekeeping magazine cover, November 1914. Photo Carole Schau.

Good *Housekeeping* magazine cover, April 1915. Photo Carole Schau.

"Between You and Me and the Lamp Post," *Life* magazine cover, December 2, 1909.

"Even the Daisies of the Field," painting for *Life* magazine cover, Easter Number, March 3, 1910.

" 'Dear' or 'Dearest'," painting for *Life* magazine cover, Furbelow Number, September 22, 1910.

"The Lure of Books," *Life* magazine cover, Book Number, June 8, 1911.

"Net Results," *Life* magazine cover, Coquette's Number, August 24, 1911. Collection Jane and Stephen Klain.

"Birches," painting for *Life* magazine cover, October 28, 1911.

Painting for *Good Housekeeping* magazine cover, November 1911.

Painting for *Life* magazine cover, Christmas Number, December 7, 1911.

Painting for *Life* magazine cover, 1912.

Painting for *Life* magazine cover, 1912.

Painting for *Good Housekeeping* magazine cover, 1913.

Painting for *Good Housekeeping* magazine cover, April 1914.

The Ladies' Home Journal magazine cover, October 1921.

FEBRUARY 16, 1922

Volume 79   Copyright, 1922, Life Publishing Company   Number 2050

PRICE 15 CENTS

"Heart to Heart," *Life* magazine cover, February 16, 1922.

"There Is a Santa Claus," *Life* magazine cover, December 1926. Collection Vincent Petragnani.

"The Call of the Wild," *Life* magazine cover, July 14, 1927 (published posthumously).

Good Housekeeping magazine covers, 1915. Photos Carole Schau.

Good Housekeeping magazine cover, September 1915.
Photo Carole Schau.

Good Housekeeping magazine cover, November 1915.
Photo Carole Schau.

Good Housekeeping magazine cover, June 1916. Photo
Carole Schau.

Good Housekeeping magazine cover, May 1917. Collection Mr. and Mrs. Joseph Suess. Photo Carole Schau.

McCall's magazine cover, June 1918. Collection Walter Kelly. Photo Carole Schau.

THE LADIES'

HOME JOURNAL

OCTOBER 1920   THE CURTIS PUBLISHING COMPANY PHILADELPHIA   TWENTY CENTS

The Ladies' Home Journal magazine cover, October 1920. Photo Carole Schau.

Life

COLES PHILLIPS

A Mere Slip of a Girl

"A Mere Slip of a Girl," *Life* magazine cover, November 18, 1920. Photo Carole Schau.

Life

"In a Position to Know," *Life* magazine cover, April 7, 1921. Photo Carole Schau.

"Memories of '83," *Life* magazine cover, 2000th issue, March 3, 1921. Collection Jane and Stephen Klain. Photo Carole Schau.

"For Divers Reasons," *Life* magazine cover, August 4, 1921. Collection Jane and Stephen Klain. Photo Carole Schau.

"The Finishing Touch," *Life* magazine cover, Vanity Number, September 29, 1921. Collection Vincent Petragnani. Photo Carole Schau.

"Bag and Baggage," *Life* magazine cover, December 15, 1921. Collection Jane and Stephen Klain. Photo Carole Schau.

Liberty magazine cover, December 5, 1925. Collection Vincent Petragnani. Photo Carole Schau.

Life magazine cover, Travel Number, April 7, 1927. Collection Jane and Stephen Klain. Photo Carole Schau.

5¢ a copy
July 2, 1927

Collier's
THE NATIONAL WEEKLY

"How to Enjoy
the Fourth"
By
H. I. Phillips

Collier's magazine cover, July 2, 1927 (published posthumously). Photo Carole Schau.

Life magazine cover, September 1, 1927 (published posthumously, the last published Phillips cover). Photo Carole Schau.

Index

Page numbers in boldface refer to illustrations.